ETSY

THE ETSY GUIDE TO SETTING UP YOUR OWN ETSY BUSINESS

Elizabeth Harrington

TABLE OF CONTENTS

Table of Contents *3*

INTRODUCTION 5

THE BIG CRAFT FAIR CONCEPT 8

BEFORE OPENING UP AN ETSY SHOP 13

TIME TO OPEN THE STORE 19

MAKING YOUR STORE SUCCESSFUL 28

COMMON MISTAKES SELLERS MAKE 34

MARKET RESEARCH 44

BUSINESS COSTS 47

CREATING YOUR PAGE 50

MARKETING 60

THE PRODUCT 62

PROMOTION 65

MARKETING YOUR PRODUCTS 66

CONVINCING A CUSTOMER THAT YOU HAVE THE BEST AND MOST UNIQUE PRODUCT 67

CHOOSING A PRICE 69

FINDING YOUR MARKET 72

CREATING A BRAND 75

GETTING TO THE TOP OF A SEARCH ENGINE 78

IMPROVING YOUR KEYWORDS 78

USING YOUR KEYWORDS 81

GETTING MORE LINKS 83

PROMOTION 87

ADVERTISING YOUR ETSY BUSINESS...............................89

SEO INTRODUCTION 92

WHAT IS SEO? 95

How does SEO work for Etsy? 103

HOW TO GET YOUR SITE SEEN.....................................112

KEEPING AHEAD OF THE GAME 115

CONCLUSION.. 118

Has anyone ever considered how many of us are craftsmen, craftswomen, artisans (or whatever term you want to use), either out of a talent that was given to us at birth, out of the family tradition that passes the art from father to son, or even out of a necessity or a hardship in our lives that needed to be resolved? How many of you know someone who does not really care about the modern manufactured goods but obsessively yearns for commodities of the past that are no longer available in commerce? How many of you own such items, or have such items in your home and just relish the idea that you kept them so that people could express their admiration and appreciation to you for insisting on keeping those artifacts alive?

In many countries, craftspeople and artisans find a solution to their need to present the fruits of their labor and their ideas through the tradition of craft fairs. In these exchange locations, there is always room for people who produce various things on their own to display and sell. Whether these are pieces of art, toys, knick-knacks, jewelry, clothing, quilts, silverware or even handmade tools, it doesn't matter. All that matters is that there is a place for these people to make their works known, appreciated and marketable.

Similarly, people who own or manufacture really unique items, especially in small quantities, and items for which collectors would pay a lot, or people who at some point acquired a few vintage items that are still sought after with an ever increasing value, need a place to present these items to the general public and perhaps get a fair exchange for them. In this last case a public fair may be impractical, especially if the unique and vintage pieces are rather bulky or very fragile.

Furthermore, fairs have a limited range of presentability. A very limited number of people visit them and even fewer really become interested in what they see. Fortunately, through the Internet, an avenue was opened for all these people to allow the much wider base of the general public to know what they have to offer and how these goods can be acquired.

Etsy was created to give a unified home to all the above. Craftsperson's and artisans from all over the world can present their creations in a single place for all the world to see. Manufacturers of really unique and limited

number items have a place to sell their products to a much wider range of markets. In a way, Etsy gave all individuals that participated in this venture the means to create their own storefront without having to incur the expenses and the capital required to open traditional or e-commerce stores of their own.

If you are a craftsman or a craftswoman, a painter or whatever else you want to call yourself, or you have a small manufacturing plant that produces unique items, you can participate in this community by setting up your own shop. In the following chapters we will be providing you with instructions and insights on how to make the most of a possible future venture in the world of Etsy.

There is one very important point that you will need to carefully consider. What kind of seller do you want to be? One that makes all of their income through this venture? Or just someone like the vast majority of the members of the community who just want to have an additional income? There will be a few options discussed on that too, to help you make the right decision.

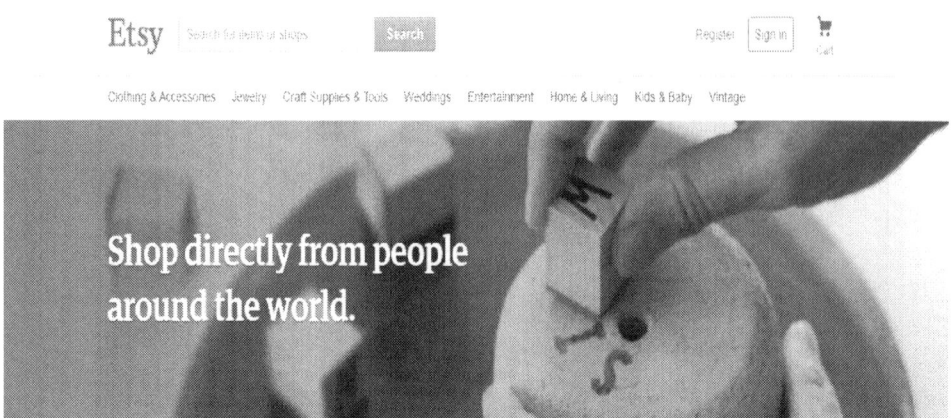

Shop directly from people around the world.

THE BIG CRAFT FAIR CONCEPT

How many of you are amateur craftsmen, musicians, painters, sculptors or any other vast variety of artist? How many of you at some point in your life learned how to create pottery but never pursued it? Curved and shaped wood? How many of you have the talent to make something out of nothing? How many of you are owners of small industries that produce handmade goods in small numbers for a limited clientele?

Such questions can reach an amount in the hundreds of thousands. There are millions if not billions of people out there who can answer yes, people who at one point or another made something out of nothing and kept it for themselves, never to be seen and appreciated by anyone else. There are almost six billion people living on this planet. To put it simply there is a potential for six billion various levels of MacGyver's out there (forgive the reference but he is the best possible example of someone who can create something out of nothing).

For those who produce small things, there is always the traditional system of craft fairs where they can put their wares in a suitcase or in the back of their car, put them on display on a stand or a table, perhaps sell a few (or a lot) and go home waiting for the next such fair. The disadvantage of this system is that even if they participated in every single fair, the clientele is limited. Most of them will never be able to travel out of their community and even if they did they probably would not be able to make it outside their country.

In those same craft fairs, people can also find items that are unique and produced by small industries as well as items that are produced by big manufacturers and have earned the title of vintage or rare. However, the same limitations apply to the people that will see and appreciate these items. Yet another limitation pertains to the bulk of the items on display. Unfortunately, the bulkiest items will never be displayed out in the open in any craft fair.

Many of the people who participate in these fairs do not care to make their livelihood out of the income produced by what they will sell. They do what they do out of love for the craftsmanship or because they just want to add a few dollars to their main income. However, many of them do want to disengage from their main work and dedicate themselves to the craftsmanship exclusively. To do that they require a much greater clientele than what they can find in the craft fairs.

The Internet and sites like Etsy provided them with the solution they needed. By creating an account in such a platform and uploading photos of their produce they were given the opportunity to present themselves to a much greater craft fair, one that spanned the entire globe and one that allowed them to open a store without having to look for the capital it would require to open a real one (which would still be limited as far as its clientele was concerned anyway!)

To avoid any misunderstandings, Etsy is not just for those that want to make their entire livelihood by selling through it. It addresses the needs of everyone who has something to sell, even if it is one single thing for a one-time transaction. This is a very handy feature for those who own really vintage items, for example an original 1957 Fender Stratocaster or an original Gibson Les Paul.

Etsy can also provide the opportunity of a cooperation which will allow a few people to get together, pool their resources and make an income out of the venture. Think about it.

Let's assume that you produce a few toys. A friend of yours produces homemade cosmetics. Your sister produces candles and a colleague produces jewelry. If each of you created your own stores you would sell x number of products and collect y amount of money. But if you all pooled your resources together and created one store, it could very well be that the total revenue could provide all four of you with a steady source of either additional or main income that would be greater than the one you would receive from separate stores.

And this is the first thing to consider. What exactly it is that you want to do. After this decision is made then it will be time to consider the five Etsy prerequisites that follow in the next chapter.

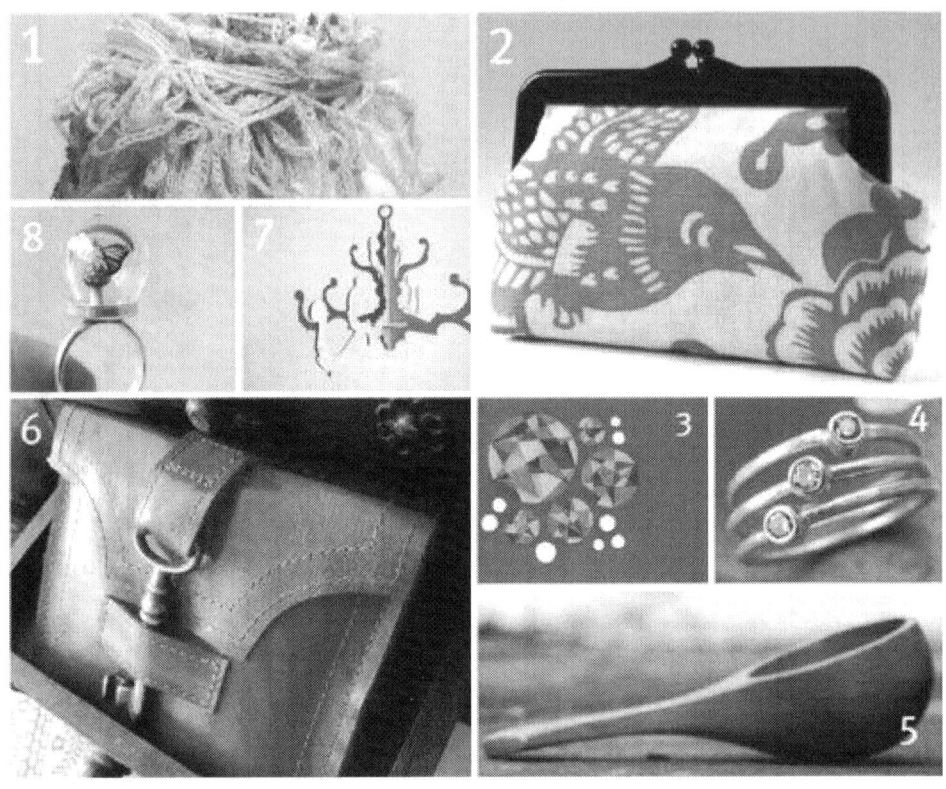

BEFORE OPENING UP AN ETSY SHOP

While the Etsy concept is pretty easy, it does not mean that creating a shop there will automatically result in filling up a bank account. Just like everything else that has to do with business and the markets, there are a number of things to consider prior to opening up this shop if you are to make an impact on the clientele you want to attract. Let's take a look at the five prerequisites:

A) **Research**

Let's assume that you are already producing something or that you have an idea of producing something new. In the first instance, every time you displayed your product or products to a local fair or to a few friends, they seemed to like what you offered, they bought it and you were left with the impression that other people might like it to.

In the second case it may not just be your idea but an observation or something that you thought of, in order to satisfy a need that you noticed people having that could not be satisfied by the available options. It could also be something that someone has suggested you should do, someone who knows about your skills and craftsmanship.

Are those enough incentives for you to open up a shop? Or was some of it just a favor to help a friend? To respond to these questions, you will need to do some research online. See if what you have to offer is sold by other people. If it is, your research will help you determine a reasonable selling price. If it is not, it would be very useful to find out why.

If there is very limited or no interest at all in your product, it may very well be that people do not know about it. If this is the case, you will need to log into a few discussion boards and find out. If this research indicates that there will be an adequate need for what you have to offer, you may proceed with opening up your shop. Otherwise you should reconsider.

B) **Something new**

Once you have completed your research and it looks favorable, i.e. people would buy what you are selling, it would be useful to check on your competition. How many other people are selling either the same thing or something similar? If you are producing unique items, the answer would be rather simple. None. If you are producing handmade items that are similar or the same as what other people sell, it is time to consider why people would show their preference to your products.

Do you offer a better craftsmanship? Is your closest competitor a thousand miles away? Do you offer faster deliveries? Are there not enough products out there to cover all the needs? The point of this exercise is to determine not only if you are going to sell but also who is going to buy. And that brings us to the next issue.

C) **Who you are addressing**

Don't kid yourself. By opening up a store at Etsy you are opening up a business of your own. One of the basic principles of business is the target market. To make this as simple as possible, the term means the individuals who, in your mind, will be interested in your products enough to buy them. You cannot open up your shop and just let it roll without a target. It will not work.

The best way to determine this target is to think of yourself. How did you become interested in the product? What prompted you? When you presented it for the first time who bought it? Do you, yourself, like this product? Would you buy this product if it was offered to you?

Answering these questions will give you the basic profile of your potential clients. Then you can extrapolate and expand based on your observations and the people who are listed as buyers of similar products from your competition.

D) **Time**

This is the really tricky part. How much time does it take you to produce what you are selling? The answer to this question will determine how much time you will be able to spend on your store. The relevant statistics show that the successful Etsy stores are those that are maintained and updated on a regular basis, i.e. there is someone spending time to do it.

If most of your time needs to be spent in your workshop, you may need to consider a partner in this venture, either to help you produce the goods faster, or to handle the store for you, especially if your knowledge about the use of the Internet is limited to browsing and downloading. It is very well known that some artists do not care for anything other than their art.

Within the time parameters you will also need to include the time it will take you to get acclimatized to the intricacies of Etsy (there are always secrets involved just like in every trade) and the time it will take you to set up your shop and make it distinguishable and quickly accessible for the buyers. Don't be hasty on this. Uploading your products with full description and photos may take quite a while, even more so if you do not have any photos already taken, or you need a fresh set.

E) **Style**

A regular mistake people make is to confuse Etsy with Amazon and e-Bay. It has nothing to do with either. Etsy has its own style and its own vibe. There have been a lot of cases where products that were very successful when traded out of an e-Bay environment did not do so well on Etsy because the shop owners did not understand the style required. When you do your research it would be very useful to roam around Etsy pages to take a look of the style involved and to get a feeling of the site.

Apart from all the above, there is one element that is important in every business venture, as well as in everything you do in life. Patience. Do not expect to sell even a single item for at least three months. For some products this may reach six months or even a year. Therefore, some persistence will be required from you in order to make your venture work.

Assuming that you considered all the above issues and the results are favorable, there is only one question to ask before proceeding any further. Do you feel confident that opening up a shop at Etsy is a good move for you? If the answer is yes, then it's time to proceed to the next chapter, which deals with the first steps of creating your shop.

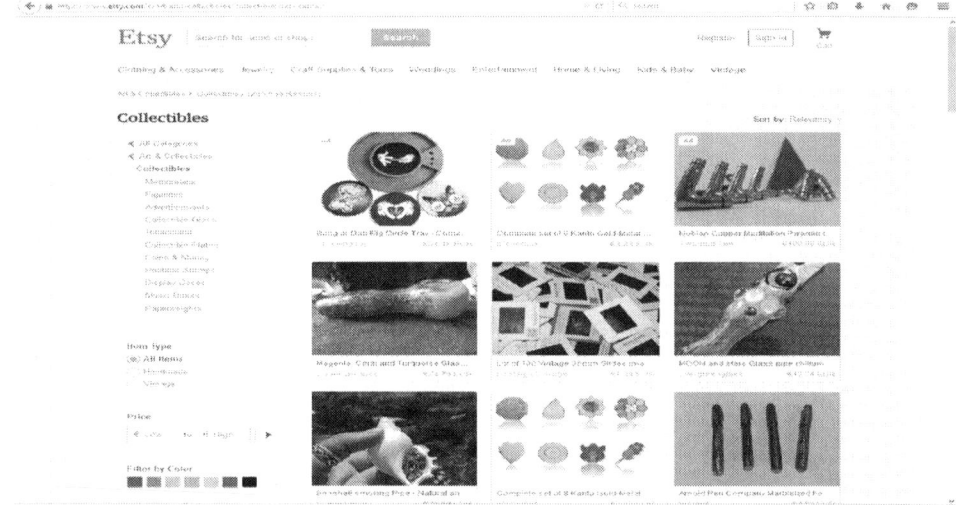

TIME TO OPEN THE STORE

So you have done your research, you have decided on what you are going to sell (it should be something that you really feel comfortable with), you found out who is going to buy it and you think that you have enough time available to devote to an Etsy store. Now what? Do you just log on to the Etsy landing page, create an account and upload photos and product descriptions? If only it could be that simple! As mentioned before, there are a few things that you need to know. Let's take a walk around these things:

A) **Learn the rules**

Etsy is not a site that lets you do whatever you want. It has guidelines and rules. For example, it does not allow resellers, and it sets specific definitions of what is considered handmade, what counts as vintage and what is deemed to belong to the category of craft supplies. Most of all it sets the rules about items that you are not allowed to sell, services you are not permitted to provide and violations that you should avoid.

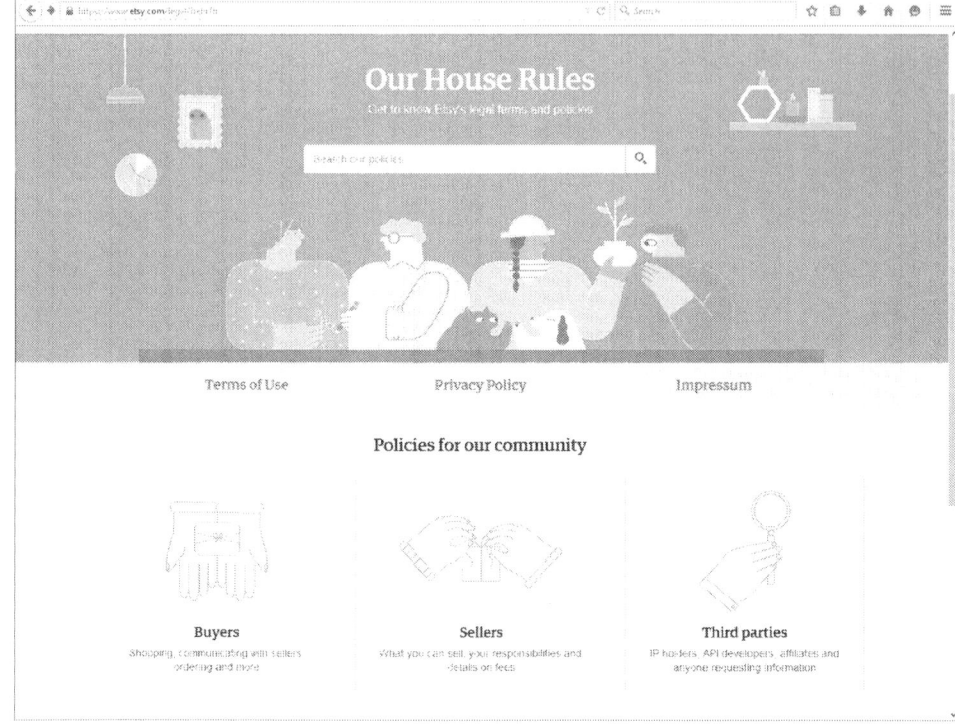

After you have carefully read and familiarized yourself with these rules it is time to proceed to the next step.

B) **Registration**

Just like any similar business site you will have to provide your name and surname, your e-mail address. You will have to choose a username and password. Needless to say, this information should be accurate and true.

C) **Select a shop name**

While you can change this later (by creating another account, not in the same one), it would be best if you have given it some thought beforehand. If people get to know you under one name, changing it later may cause people to think that you either sold out, or you are changing something significant and therefore they will have to re-evaluate you.

Most people choose names with personal significance or names that represent the products they upload. This is the easy way out, not to mention that you could run into other stores with the same name. What you actually need to do is:

- Choose a name that does not look like an e-mail or can be interpreted as an account handle or a chat room
- Think of a name that you would use for a regular brick and mortar store
- Think of an open-ended name that will allow you to change your product inventory without significant problems
- Think of a name that is distinctive enough, unique if possible (search to see if there is anything even close to it), easy to remember and not too difficult to type in the search box

- Avoid using numbers or long words.

D) **Banner and avatar**

As the popular saying goes, an image is worth 1,000 words. The banner that you will select is the first thing that your potential buyers will see. At a resolution of 760 x 100 pixels, 72 px/inch that Etsy has set for the banners, you need to incorporate the elements that represent your shop and that catch the eye. Etsy provides an app that you can use, or you can use the graphic software of your preference to create this banner.

In a similar manner, the avatar is used to identify your store and by extension, you. Even though it is a smaller image in size, it should incorporate the same characteristics as the banner.

E) **The profile**

Now we have reached the heart and soul of your store. Your profile is what will persuade the vast majority of the buyers to purchase your products. It needs to be convincing, professional, accurate, precise, concise, in a logical progression, and personal enough so that people can relate to you. The profile will only be disregarded if what you offer is so unique and sought after that the buyers will not even care who they are dealing with.

You cannot deviate in the policies listed in your profile from the policies of Etsy. If you have more than one user account, you need to list them all. If more than one person handles the store, you need to list each name and job title, and their primary responsibilities, in very few words.

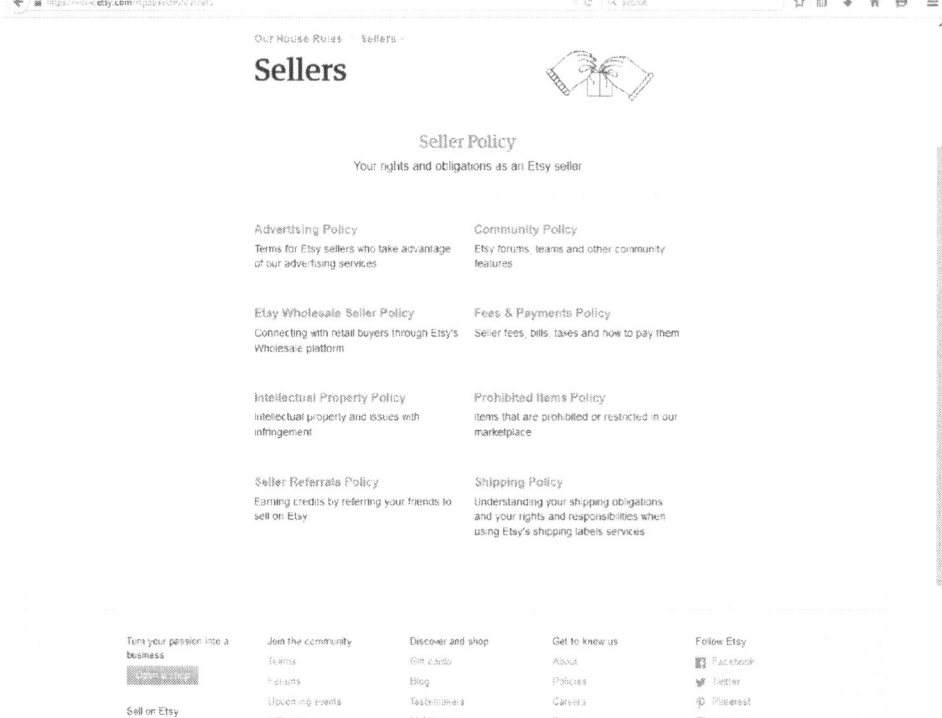

Always keep in mind the basic rule of a profile in an Internet site. It shows that you care and that you mean business. An incomplete profile shows hastiness and lack of interest. A profile that provides no information at all will be disregarded. Therefore, it's in your best interest to not only complete your profile but also complete it in a way that shows that you are SERIOUS about what you are doing.

F)   **The products**

This is the part that could consume a considerable amount of time if you have a lot of products to include. Each product should be uploaded with a captive photo so people can see exactly what they are buying, as well as a full description, the price and a careful selection of keywords. This is the way your buyers are going to find it and consequently find you and your store.

Welcome to Etsy, where you can discover over **15 million** unique handmade and vintage items from over **800,000** independent, creative businesses in over **150** countries.

Similar Items See more

Wooden Geometric Vase M   Wooden Bowl 12" Neon Pin.   Wooden Nesting Bowls set o.   Small Wooden Clock Mixer   Double Time Clock MIMOZA
UrbanAnalog $30.00 usp   infuturedIW $67.00 usp   WindkreisU $145.00 usp   weasupphone $78.00 usd   aidasnomune $82.00 usp

Home › UrbanAnalog › Candle Holders

Like this Item ?
♡ Favorite   Add it to your favorites to revisit it later.

$46.50 USD   Only 1 available

Add to Cart

♡ Favorite

Geometric Wood Candlesticks - Polyhedron Origami Inspired Design

Shop

UrbanAnalog
Mirrors, Candlesticks, Modern & Vintage Home Accessories.

8 Items

♡ Add shop to favorites
☆ See who favorites this shop

Shop owner

UrbanAnalog
Marquette, Michigan,
United States

Favorites
Circle
Feedback 55, 100% pos.

Contact

Item

♡ Add item to favorites
☆ See who favorites this item

Tweet   Pin it   Like 19

For the modern table top, these Origami-like candlestick holders are constructed from a solid sheet of maple wood veneer. Each holds a standard size taper candlestick. Please note the candleholders do not come with the candlesticks as shown in photo.

Materials
The geometric pattern is precision cut, scored, and then folded to assemble around a solid interior structure of laser cut acrylic. We then finish the wood surface with a coat of durable satin clear poly urethane.

Now that we have covered the basics, it's time to consider the issues that separate the wheat from the chaff, details that can lead to a successful business with high standards and strong brand names. Many of you will question the necessity of going to all this trouble if you are only interested in making an additional income out of the endeavor.

The reason is simple. People always prefer to buy from stores that are well maintained, even over the Internet. If your store is not properly managed, then you will not be able to make the additional income you want. This will be discussed further in the next chapter.

MAKING YOUR STORE SUCCESSFUL

Every trade has its secrets that lead to success. Online stores have their secrets too. Etsy is not all that different from an online store that you would create and operate completely on your own. The same principles apply and the same strategies and tactics are needed in order to make any online shop successful. The proven course of action includes:

A) **Making a task list depending on your goals**

A frequent mistake sellers make in Etsy is to upload everything right from the start. This is wrong on many levels. They think that with a greater number of products they can increase their sales. They could not be more wrong. It's a matter of goals.

If your goal is to make a sale in three months, then you need to focus and upload those products that you have found after your research to be the most sought after. Make sure their descriptions are accurate, the photos are accurate and eye catching, and the price is right. A product that is not requested all that much may take up to a year to sell the first time; therefore, it can be uploaded later.

Remember that every time you upload a new product, your store is updated and upgraded. If you do that right from the start, people will become accustomed to the changes and be more prone to return to the site on a regular basis. As mentioned before, the most successful shops are those with an active owner, always looking to improve and fine tune their store.

What you need to do is create a task list. "This week I'll upload product A and product B, next week I'll upload products C and D. In the meantime, I must check if my competition modified their prices to match mine", etc...

Set your milestones and follow them. However, this should not exclude a modification in the case conditions change. If, for example, your first product did not make it as opposed to the second, which made a killing, you need to shift your focus from the first product to the second and even take the first product down altogether. While the task list is imperative, it should not be restrictive. Forming a business is not about rigidness. You stick to your objectives but you do so with flexibility and adaptability to the unexpected or unanticipated.

B) **Select your keywords carefully**

All search engines work under the same principle. The user enters a word or a phrase and they search for the matching ones in the various sites. Etsy's search engine works in exactly the same way. The buyers enter a search parameter of what they want to buy and then if your keywords match the search parameter, your shop appears on the list of results.

While the same principles of search engine optimization that work for Google would work here as well, let's stick to the basics that everyone can understand. In the listings editor, Etsy allows you to tag your products with keywords. Think about the keywords that you would use to search for your own products and plug them in. Brainstorm even more and select the ones that you think are the strongest. Use the same keywords and phrases in your titles and your descriptions.

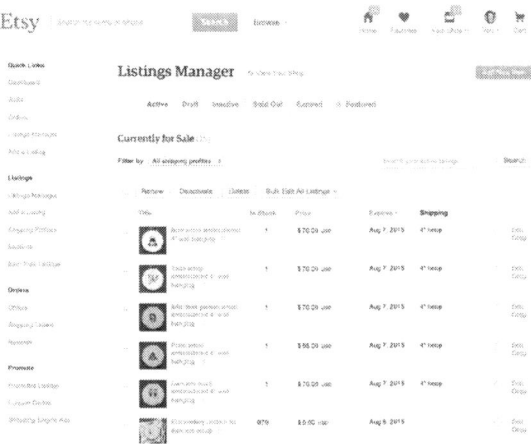

A very useful tool that Etsy offers you is the Shop Stats. It shows you which keywords and key phrases worked and which didn't. Replace the ones that didn't.

C) It's all in the photos

Many online stores warn that the product photos are only indicative and that the actual product delivered may be different from the product shown in the photo. In the finer points of marketing this is a great mistake. You must make sure that the photos you upload for your products always match the product that you sell. If you manufacture green pairs of shoes and suddenly you run out of stock or you decide to manufacture red ones instead, replace the picture to show the red ones.

Uploading the correct picture is mostly a matter of trust. Think about the following situation. You kept the green picture for your shoes. You posted a written notice that said "Green shoes exhausted, only red ones available!" Your client placed an order but did not see the warning. You send the red shoes and the delivery was accepted. While the transaction was complete and it earned you money, how would you feel with the following review: "I thought I was ordering the green shoes. He posted the warning but I didn't notice it so I was disappointed to receive the red shoes." Is this a positive review? Will this client buy from you again?

D) Focus on conversion, not perfection

The point of the exercise is to sell the products. It is useful to present the products in the best way possible but you should not hold a product back if you feel that the presentation is not perfect. Upload your product, decide on a competitive price, make sure that the photo is correct and that the description is accurate, and let it sell. You will have plenty of opportunity to come back to it later and revise whatever you want.

There are plenty of cases where people are not interested in the description at all. They are just happy to find the product they have been looking for at the price they are willing to pay. You should not miss the opportunity because you did not upload the product due to the imperfection of its presentation.

E) **Make sure that you can deliver on what you promise**

This is why it is important to divide your time wisely. When you have uploaded a product you need to be sure that the product is available for sale. Remember that a store works on stock. You have the advantage of not waiting for a manufacturer to send you products to replenish your stock. If you do not have a product in stock, take it down until it is time to get down to your workshop and manufacture more.

Similarly, if you state that you will deliver a product in 5 days, make sure that the service you use for the deliveries will do so. It would be best if you allowed yourself some leeway and mentioned 5 to 7 days instead of 5. It's also a smart idea to make sure the delivery of the goods is professionally handled by your delivery service.

However, the most important issue here is that you maintain the proper contact with your client. If something goes wrong, for any reason, advise them immediately of the situation and offer an alternative.

So far we have discussed what you should know and do when you decide to open up a store on Etsy. Now it's time to discuss what you should not do.

COMMON MISTAKES SELLERS MAKE

The basic principles of doing business are known to almost everyone. Even as employees, people learn from the tactics and strategies of their employers, especially if they are successful. However, there are always issues that remain confidential and are not revealed even to the employees to maintain the aspect of job security. While some of your tactics can be of your own design (many people think that their way is always the best), there are some tactics and some situations that you must avoid.

A) **Always check the details**

This is a very frequent mistake that comes from an over load of work, and being too hasty. Never send a package anywhere without double checking the details, especially if there are any comments that your client wrote. Do not assume that PA means Pennsylvania. It can just as easily mean Patras!

If there is a typo or something that does not make sense, don't be shy -- ask for clarification. If there is something puzzling you in the order, do not be afraid to ask for confirmation.

It is always nice to sit amongst friends and tell jokes about someone who ordered a hammer and got a pair of scissors instead. Or how a package that should have gone to Alaska ended up in Albuquerque.

It's funny only for those who listen to it, not for the client that suffered the mistake and not for you who may have lost a client due to this mistake.

B) **Ship your items smartly**

Products must arrive at their destination in one piece. It would be of no use to anyone if a unique vintage product arrived in its destination shattered to pieces. Personally I would be furious if I ordered a 1957 Fender Precision Bass and it arrived with the neck separated from the body, the strings broken and the pick guard hanging out of the body! I would require compensation immediately and it wouldn't matter to me whose fault it would be, especially for a product that I would have spent thousands of dollars!

This is where we must make a very important remark. By law the entity that is held liable for such incidents is the company that the buyer bought the product from and that means you. I.e. if there are any amends to be made and any compensations to be given, those will come out of your hide!

It is your responsibility to make sure that everything you ship is packaged smartly and with ample provisions so that your product arrives safely at its destination regardless of what the transport company will do. Never assume that any delivery company handles things with care. They don't.

C) **Do not underprice your products**

This is not just a matter of making a reasonable profit, not even a matter of not getting paid for the time you spent creating the product. Just like a few other issues, it's a matter of trust. When the products from China first made their appearance worldwide, people did not trust them at all because of their low prices and they did not buy them.

The situation changed after the general public was informed of the very low wages the workers are paid, which justifies the low commercial prices. Then the question became a moral one. The point is, had this information not become public knowledge, people would still not buy Chinese products.

Everyone knows how much work is put into a homemade product. And everyone values a homemade product exactly because it's homemade. Automatically, in their minds this means a higher price. Low prices immediately turn the mind to machine made products. And this is why they do not trust an underpriced product.

The usual mistake is to see how much others charge and either charge the same or something a little lower. That's not the way to do it. You need to see how much you are paying for the raw materials, how much you are paying for the electric bills, how much you are paying to replace your tools before making a decision on the price's sweet spot which will bring you sales and income.

D) **Think like a customer**

You need to step out of yourself. The general rule of thumb when writing descriptions and providing information is to think what the people reading them really want to know. What seems to you as an obvious detail that could be omitted does not mean that other people consider it so. Every detail counts and not everyone has the same mental capability to understand nuances.

If you are selling things for kids, think like a parent with children, even if you do not have any. If you are selling musical instruments, think like a musician. One of the greatest mistakes you can make, and one you should avoid at all costs, is to write those descriptions as yourself. If necessary, ask someone relevant to the product that you want to sell to tell you what would likely be read in the description and the other tags.

E) **Avoid offensive products**

A regular mistake sellers make is failing to pay attention to the nature of what they sell. It may seem innocuous to you, but to some it may be insulting. The issue does not actually involve sexually explicit material. It also includes products that can induce issues of racism, gender or sexual preference discriminations and religious offenses.

This issue is, in fact, an ambiguity. What is offensive and what isn't? What religious fanatics consider as offensive to their religion, for other people it may be considered as freedom of speech and expression. Such differences are the ones that led to the Charlie Hebdo incident. Similarly, a shirt with a crying bear ironed on cannot be considered as violating the rights of animals as many activists lately maintain.

This issue is completely at your discretion. It's our advice that moderation and considerate thinking are required. It is possible that more extreme products will sell more. But they will also cause you more problems. If you decide to go for more extreme options, you should declare it in your profile so that people will have an idea what to expect when they browse through your products. A relevant warning could also save you some trouble with negative reviews.

F) **Always respond**

No matter how carefully you prepare your descriptions, people will always have questions. As mentioned already, different individuals perceive things in different ways. Many sellers neglect to respond to questions they consider trivial or to questions that have been answered in the presentation of the product. Even worse, they respond with an insulting, "Read the description" sentence.

That's a great mistake and should be avoided. Sometimes people already know the answer to the question they pose. They pose it to see if you will respond at all and to check the level of your professionalism. No response or an insulting response will cost you the customer. Make it a point to pay attention to every single question and respond accordingly.

G) **Always publish your reviews or ratings**

Unless you are a new seller, people will be looking to see what other people are saying about you and how they value your way of doing business. The positive reviews are always welcome and valuable but you can gain even more with a negative review that has been successfully responded to.

Never underestimate the power of a good response to a negative comment. That's an even worse mistake than not responding to the negative comment at all. You may not be able to respond to a negative rating, but you can see to it that it is not repeated.

H) **Do not avoid the seller protection program**
On occasion there will be problems with your financial transactions. It does not matter whose fault it is. What matters is that without this protection the error will be reflected in the status of your account and the consequences could range from great to disastrous.

The last issue to consider, if you are a resident of a country that is a member of the European Union, is that Etsy will withhold the amounts that pertain to the Value Added Tax that are applicable to all the member states, and send it to the appropriate tax authorities in your name. This means that you may not have to take any action to declare this amount to the appropriate tax revenue systems but you will have to declare the income through your sales from your Etsy shop. Otherwise there will be no correlation with the taxes remitted with your name and you will be accused of tax evasion.

Etsy provides a platform that makes it easy for everyone to start their own shop and start earning money out of it. No money has to be spent to site designers, no capital is needed for advertisement and no salaries have to be paid to professional marketers and SEO specialists, and no amounts of money have to go to purchasing the first stock. That's a lot of money to save. However, you will have to supply the products, abide by the rules and follow some simple guidelines to generate an income for yourself.

MARKET RESEARCH

The first thing you should do when starting any enterprise is to do a bit of firsthand research, and do it with an open mind. It is surprising how many businesses decide not to do this and instead just start operating, fueled entirely from the good feelings a new business gives and they just fill in the blanks when they've failed. Begin by going on Etsy and looking around, not just products you are interested in buying and selling, but everything on offer. Try to use the site as though you are the most useless Internet user on the web and you are just trying to find something cool to buy for yourself, or as a gift. How do different products get presented to you? How does the seller's profile influence you? What keeps coming to the top and what really puts you off a product?

The biggest obstacle many beginners face with a business like this is that they assume because they have an interesting product it will sell itself, and they ignore how they find interesting new products themselves. Try making a simple chart that will show how you got from the front page to an item you liked and you were ready to buy because this will tell you a lot. You might begin by typing 'shoes' into the search bar, then you might refine the categories, and choose 'handmade' and change the price range. You might then find you start trying new terms like 'size 8' or 'boots'. What about when you click on the profile? What do you look to then? Perhaps the image of the seller puts them at odds with the brand. Maybe the description is too funky and some of the reviews sound obviously fake or make you realize the shoes are being mostly bought by older women.

Later you will have a better understanding of how to change these things yourself but for now it is fundamental that you understand what gets you from the front page to the checkout. After playing with it for a while you should understand quite well how you find different products and what makes a product appealing. This is when you should start turning towards making your own page and starting on a business plan.

BUSINESS COSTS

Luckily Etsy has no membership fee for signing up and it makes its money from taking a 3.5% bite out of the cost of your sale, which considering the service it actually provides is not a huge amount. There is also a small 20 cent fee for every 4 months that an individual product is listed (that is you'd have to pay it again if it didn't sell in 4 months). This is not a huge amount but it can add up: every 50 products you list will cost you $10 and you haven't made anything until they've sold. If you are planning on selling lots of small products, be sure they will sell or that your overall profits are high enough to easily absorb those kinds of costs. It might also be worth selling multiple products at once if they can be bundled together.

When making a business plan, remember the costs for when you are making a product to figure out the profit – this is something many beginners can overlook. Let's say you make paintings of ducks to sell on Etsy. You use 20¢ worth of paint, the canvas costs you $3, it takes two hours of your time which is worth $20, the packaging and shipping costs $5, and the listing costs 20¢, which means it costs you $28.40 to make and list the product, and you'll need to add 99¢ for Etsy's fee meaning you have to make more than $29.39 to make a profit on that painting. You will also need to advertise the product, monitor your products, and respond to questions about the product.

Before starting with Etsy and figuring out the secrets to success make sure that you can make some actual money from selling your product at a price people will buy. No matter how much you sell, it doesn't matter if you don't make a significant profit in the end. The main cost to look at for something like Etsy is how much you get an hour. Some people will be able to make many products in an hour and other people will not mind working for a low wage per hour if they get to do what they enjoy without the stress of a hectic work environment. It might be hard to come up with a number for your cost per product, because you are most likely the main laborer behind the product so your wage is what you can get for the product.

It is good to work backwards from how much you need to make or potentially what you would be worth if you were employed. If you know it takes you one hour to make a pair of earrings and you have 15 hours a week to make earrings, then you know you could make approximately 750 earrings a year for 50 weeks of work. You then need to figure out the cost you need to make a year just to make the venture worthwhile – this is not how much profit you think you can make but just the simple minimum that you would be comfortable with making. For some, Etsy is a valuable learning experience or a means for boosting your CV, so a lower amount is acceptable. For others they would need to earn at least minimum wage. You might like to consider how much you would pay someone else to do this level of work. If you get to say $5000 a year, then for 750 hours of work you would find your labor worth $6.60 per earring.

For a lot of people working on their own, the cost of their labor and the profit are going to be the same thing and on a small scale it is fine to think like that, but when you are actually trying to make money you do have to consider what your time is worth versus finding another source of income. The reason for this is that you need to place a value on your product and without including the cost of your work in that, you might be under the impression you are making more than you really are. It is a very common rookie mistake to think that your time costs you nothing.

CREATING YOUR PAGE

With the previous two exercises you should have a rough idea of how much products like your sell for on Etsy and also how much you can make with your product. Don't assume that because other people are on Etsy selling a similar product at a certain price that they must be making a profit so you'll be fine as well.

If you have decided you can make money and you are happy with the work you need to put in, then you are now ready to start signing up and creating your page. The following sections will give you design tips and how to sell yourself, but this section will give you a quick guide to just signing up to Etsy. Getting a basic account is simple. Just enter in the usual information you gave up trying to hide from internet spies a long time ago and click send. You will need to upgrade to a seller's account which will require a credit card – there is not really any way around that in the USA even if you accept payment via other means (other countries may be able to sign up with PayPal).

Listings

Signing up is set up as 'opening a store' and the site encourages you to choose a name and start listing items before you've even tweaked with the settings. You will need to list at least one or two items before you can move on with the process but don't worry too much at this point. Just get familiar with the process and put an item up – you can change it later as well as your name.

Since you need to begin with a listing it is worth discussing how listings work and the kinds of items you can put up on Etsy, as it will let you see the mechanics of the site and let you understand how the rest of it will work. Many items are allowed to be sold on Etsy – the only ones outright prohibited, that are likely to be relevant, are those made from things like Ivory or the pelt of a dodo, and items that infringe copyright which you might encounter if you are making print designs or similar. You can sell both physical and digital items if you like – this might mean selling something like a photograph print or a kit for making a scrapbook. Remember though that things on Etsy must be handmade by you or someone you are affiliated with, or they must be vintage (at least 20 years old), or they must be some kind of craft supply.

If it is homemade you must be able describe the people who have made the item and ideally you or your business must have made the item. It is against Etsy's rules to resell things – they must be original in some way even if you have just designed the item. One of the things that sets Etsy apart from other sites is that the images of products have to be of the item you are selling (no stock photos) and you need to make it clear if you are using one photo for lots of similar items that what the buyer gets might vary from what is in the photo. In addition, they must be your own photos that are natural without any naughty photo shopping of blemishes. They also say your profile and about section must be honest but this is 'business' honest rather than normal honest, so you can still spruce up the truth a little and not admit you make your products in your pants.

The Photograph

The photograph might be the single most important feature of what sells your product – it may even work to sell a less than brilliant product. You probably know from your own shopping around on the site that you'd never pick up a product that had the cheap, flash-on crumpled-shirt hung over the back of a door look that eBay favors. However, with a half-decent camera, some basic lightning, an arty arrangement, and perhaps a filter to make up for it all and your product will look good.

To begin with, a smartphone should be okay for pictures, but you will want to upgrade to something with more stopping power soon. In terms of lighting, you will probably want to stick to lots of natural light from a window and have a clean work surface to place an item on or some interesting but relevant backdrop. Many items do well if you hang them in front of a white wall.

 At the right time of day there will not be too much shadow and you can't go too wrong with a white background (try some printer paper if that is all you have). You can have several pictures up so feel free to play with distance and depth of focus but don't go so arty that you put people off by not showing them the product. Try to give a good indication of how big a product is (put them on furniture people can recognize) and seriously consider a human model with clothing or jewelry. It is usually a good idea to play with a photograph once you have it on your computer. Free programs like Google's Picasa will let you crop an image and it has easy-to-use sliders for tweaking the shadows and lighting.

The Description

Descriptions of products are more important than you might think since we come across a lot and we tend to skim over them. Descriptions that are poorly written or shot full of errors will turn off prospective buyers that only have your words to really judge you on. Many people work very hard on making their products and then stick an ugly little description that doesn't convey any of the passion they have for it – or even try to properly sell it. You needn't pull a Shakespeare on anyone though, just make sure that you have all of the salient information and that you start with the most important information first. If I have to ask a question about the size, the material, how to use something etc. then most likely I'll move on or by the time you've replied I've bought something else. Make a note of questions you get asked and think of information you might want to know to include.

When writing a description make sure to format it nicely for reading, with bullet points and short paragraphs, and ensure that you keep it all relevant to the product. Some basic rules of writing copy come in handy: things are never old they are rustic, worn is stressed, and a simple design is minimalist. Don't forget to mention any interesting selling points that might not be immediately obvious and consider mentioning ideas about what you can do with the product: a dress might be well paired with a certain type of shoe and might be suitable for an interview or a night out. People sometimes like a little story at Etsy – a quick sentence about your inspiration and any personal touches about your relationship to the product. If it's vintage and you have an interesting story people will love it, especially if you can spin it to sound exciting, but avoid saying you found it in the attic of an elderly neighbor who just died.

Later in the book there will be a basic guide to promoting your site with keywords and search engine optimization but try to be mindful of keywords already, and be clever with the naming of the product so that it is short but something people will search. At the end of the article have a link to other products or parts of Etsy they might be interested in. Make sure to keep coming back and editing your description.

Tags, Categories and Materials

The last pieces of the listing puzzle are the extras you have to include on a listing that make it searchable on Etsy, which is possibly the main way people will find your products. It is useful to know which tags are the most used and you can look at the analytics on your page to see how people are actually finding your products (more on this later). For now, it is important to consider what it is you are selling in broad terms: a shoe, the specific type of thing that it is: a trench boot, your audience: teenage girls, what it is made of, the color, the size, its uses: kitchenware, its size, the era it is from and the occasion it might be used for: weddings, birthdays. The categories your product falls into should come quite naturally depending on whether they are handmade or vintage and what color they are.

It is important that your tags and materials do not falsely represent what it is you are selling by using colors that are not quite correct or by using synonyms for materials that could be misleading. It's not likely you will get in trouble but it is against official Etsy policy. Try to make sure that any tags you use are going to be the most obvious for someone using a search engine and you don't use 'burnt umber' where you could use 'brown'. People have gotten very used to thinking in keywords so that people simply type in things like 'wedding shoe 9' and they don't waste words – so don't waste yours. After a while you will refine this and have the best tags you can.

The About Section

Your products make you on Etsy – it's like any other store in that respect. If they look good and sound good, then your page will automatically be filled with inviting looking morsels that will keep people clicking on your profile and coming back. Etsy, unlike a lot of stores in the world now, still manages to maintain something of a small town feel though and who you are is quite important in the community. You are not guaranteed to get more sales by paying attention to your image but it is important to try and take in the Etsy ethos. People are looking to be sold a product and with unique objects that are the foundation of Etsy they want a story. If you make necklaces out of shells they want to know that you waggle them out of the sand on the beaches of California once a week. If you're a traditional boot cobbler from outback Texas this is something your buyers will enjoy telling to the people they are giving the boots as a gift to. Even if you just run a market stall from the hallowed punk grounds of Camden, London people will want to know

A good about section does a few things: it gives you credibility and justifies your prices; it reassures buyers you are not just in it for the money but that you love your craft, and it gives them a reason to connect with you and share you with their friends. An empty profile says you are just in this for a quick buck, but even if you are, make those bucks even quicker. You can put up a banner and a portfolio picture and you should take care to put a good quality image that conveys a sense you are creative, colorful and respectable. If you are afraid to put up a photo of yourself then a picture of a logo or something similar is fine in this instance. A picture of you is good, especially if you are in your studio (maybe put on a bit of a costume) and you are surrounded by your other creations. Include pictures of how you make the product and the studio you make it in.

The about page also lets you add pictures of people who work with you and you can have photos of them so we simpletons viewing will imagine you as elves tinkering away at the product we want to buy. It can be strangely tedious to fill out these things but it rarely takes more than an hour or so and any business will likely need lots of photos of themselves anyway. It is important, though, because it makes it seem as though you have been around for a while and you are not waiting to see how it goes before you make a real effort. As for writing the about page, don't over think it or worry too much. Try to be honest, tell your story and give any interesting information about your product. Include information about the materials you use and how you get them. Don't concern yourself about sounding incredibly professional or artistic because people are looking for authenticity here. If you are struggling just sit down and write your story with no intention of publishing it to the site and from there take out the best bits.

Your Page

You should have some good ideas about how to set up your page and how to get your listings looking fantastic. With your pricing sorted and people now able to buy your products and see who you are then you are already on your way to Etsy success. There are many other facets of signing up to Etsy, so many that to answer lots of small questions would take too long to effectively cover and Etsy is a well-designed site with a lot of information ready to help you. What you need to know now is how to market your product and take your sales to the next level.

MARKETING

With Etsy, marketing is everything. That's not an understatement because many of the traditional roles of a business are taken over by Etsy or they are eaten up by marketing. Maintaining the site, looking after accounts, and the sale of the product will all be handled, more-or-less, by Etsy. You are most likely working for yourself so you don't need to worry about managing other employees or making sure they're not stealing your products. Customer service is still very important and you will need to make sure everything is sent out on time and you respond well to any queries, but even here it's best to think of customer service as another branch of your marketing.

With Etsy you make an excellent product and then you market it. The only thing left is shipping it off. Marketing covers a lot of things, you already dabbled with it in designing your profile and listing your products, but you need to take it further so that you are being active instead of just casting bait into a search engine and hoping it attracts something. You need to make sure that your product is either on trend or made to be, you need to make sure you are getting up to the top of a search engine (and yes, you can get your Etsy page on Google), you need to make sure that you are connecting with a wider community and actively recommending your product to people, and you need to get your product seen by those who matter. Nearly all of the rest of this book will be about marketing, but as I've said, there's not much else to it.

THE PRODUCT

Marketing begins with your product. Let me ask you, what are you intending to sell? A nice pair of leather boots? Wrong, you are selling 1920s kidskin riding boots worn by prospectors and made by a master craftsman in Tennessee. What I'm saying is that your product isn't what you are selling but the perception you make of it. On sites like Etsy people rarely just look at one thing then buy it and leave. They like to browse and so you have a chance to sell. Having the best product is irrelevant a lot of the time and having a genuinely unique one is as well. It's about making it look unique.

Leather and Italian leather is the same thing but which are you going to pick? Beef stew can be found anywhere in the British Isles but in America it will always be sold as Irish stew for almost no reason except that it sets it apart. You are limited on Etsy about how much you can build your brand but you can make sure that there is something that differentiates your product from another one even if it is no different. Try to pick a thing you haven't seen and then make that your thing – whether that is a material, pattern, style, era or location. You can't beat a huge brand in the sneaker market because Nike has that covered but you can be number one in a category that you made up such as vegan sneakers made out of hemp. You can't be ridiculous with this but make sure to know which category you want your product to be in.

You may also have been wondering what your product should sell or where should you expand. If you just make a single product, then a lot of Etsy marketing might be a waste of time because people aren't necessarily going to keep buying the same product. You might have come into this book hoping to find some inspiration because you like making things but you don't know what make yet. The key, in that case, is finding what is trending and then finding a new category you can make, building a brand around that and making products with excellent margins (that are hopefully easy to ship).

Etsy has a page for trending products called Trend watch which will help a bit. Sites like Twitter, Buzzfeed and Google all have features for looking at what people are looking up. If you set up alerts and pay attention to Twitter that will be helpful. You really want to find what Amazon, eBay and Pinterest are trending and make sure to follow a few craft and design blogs and magazines. Don't blindly follow what people are into but also don't wait around for something to die. It's often good to springboard from one idea to something else. Are people making miniature letters you can send to friends? What else could you make that is miniature?

Once you have thought about these options you will want to start making new and quality products that stick to a theme or ethos that you have to make sure people come back to you. Perhaps try always using a certain material that people like whether that is because it is authentic or because you only use organic materials. You can then try becoming a voice in that field among bloggers and keep growing in that way so you know about new developments and people will start turning to your products after listening to what you have to say.

You've got a product that stands out, it's packaged nicely and you know you can make a good bit of money if you can just get them sold. What you need to focus on now is getting the product seen in the huge sea of Etsy. Putting your unique spin on trending products and being careful with tags and materials is a start that will raise your prospects but you want to get further up in the search engine both on Etsy and on engines like Google. You also want people to have a reason to come across your product without directly looking for something like this. The remainder of this book will be split between increasing your product's searchability on Etsy and reaching out to the community and getting your name heard in the online world.

MARKETING YOUR PRODUCTS

There are some universal rules of marketing that apply to all products that you can sell, but in a more casual marketplace environment like Etsy it might not seem like you would need to apply those same tactics, but you would be completely wrong. The basic rules of marketing still apply -- you have to make a customer believe that your product, and no one else's, is the one for them and it is worth the price you are asking. That seems obvious until you break it down further. Let's say you are selling some leather boots. Your customer has to believe that you are selling the best boots (you might not be) and that you are selling unique boots (they might not be). The question is, how do you get a customer to believe that.

CONVINCING A CUSTOMER THAT YOU HAVE THE BEST AND MOST UNIQUE PRODUCT

What do we mean when we say, "I am selling the best product"? Do we mean you are selling the best boots in the world? Of course not, that is an impossible task in a world where there are twice as many boots as there are people to buy them. You need to be the best at selling your product, which means you have to define what that product is. You can't have the best leather boots but you can have the best rainbow colored crocodile leather boots. The key here is in understanding what it is that is unique about your product, regardless whether it is particularly unique or not. You have to choose the category where your product will sell the best.

The beauty of Etsy is that it thrives on originality and you will probably have something interesting about your product, either in the way you make it or in the type of product that it is. If you make furniture out of old wooden pallets from a supermarket, then that is your selling point; if you make boots using a traditional method from your part of the world then that is your selling point; if you make earrings out of potatoes, then that is your selling point. When you have a unique angle, you can be the best in that particular niche and suddenly you've dramatically reduced your competition.

There is a sense in which marketing like this can seem futile in a selling format like Etsy, because people browse, and will click on the things they like, not what you've told them to like. However, remember that people have to search for a product on Etsy and while it is difficult to come up first on the list for boots, it is possible to come up first if you have a more unique product. With Etsy you can find several different angles and sell your products that way. One pair of boots could sell because they are Spanish leather, because they are traditionally made, because they are custom treated, because they are dress boots, or because they are good for winter.

When you have something really unique, then focus on that uniqueness when promoting your product in other markets to sell on Etsy. If you share your products on Pinterest, blogs or forums, remember to be consistent. You want to be the person that makes one thing very well. If you want to make other things out of Spanish leather that is fine, but it is better to do that than to have one hundred types of boots with no real selling points other than being nice boots. Think of some of your favorite brands and how they actually sell their products. You know Nike as a brand that sells good quality sport shoes; you don't want to buy fashion boots from them. You know Ugg boots because they sell wooly sheepskin boots. You might buy other sheepskin products from Ugg or boots with a similar design, but a general audience is not going to be interested in a pair of regular cow leather work shoes from Ugg. Once you have a big enough brand and marketplace, then you can sell almost anything you like with some success. Be aware of how these businesses grew themselves because that is where you are now.

Later you will learn how to implement this branding and marketing into your product and promotion, but for now write down some ideas that make your product unique and appealing in a way that competitors currently are not doing. Try to stick to this idea in what you do in the future.

CHOOSING A PRICE

Finding a category where you are the best is only one small part of marketing and selling. Another key issue is pricing. Pricing tells a customer how much a product is worth to you to make (if you can sell it cheap, then it is cheap) and it lets them know who it is targeted towards (if it's cheap then it's not high fashion). You need to know how to competitively price yourself on Etsy.

Since you should have, or will be working on, a business plan, you should have a reasonable idea about what your time is worth and what the cost of production is. You should also have a good idea how much you need to sell it for in order to make a reasonable profit after the Etsy's costs. You need to keep in mind how much experience you have (you could be working for someone else for a lot more money) and other invisible costs such as time spent reading up on marketing. Business gurus often recommend that you spend at least a few hours a week promoting your product. You cannot just view marketing and promotion as a small task you do once every so often that doesn't really cost you anything.

When it comes to actually pricing your product to sell, things become more complex, including depending on previous experience, trial and error, and how much money you are content to make per hour of your time. Take a look at your competition...all of it. Write down the prices of at least 30 products, and if there is enough diversity you will have to look at even more. This won't take long and then you will have a good idea of what you should charge. If you have terrible photos and a poorly constructed page, with a high price tag, people will not trust you. Research should tell you which criteria dictate what people choose to charge. Try to experiment with price but remember you cannot alter it too much when people are paying attention. Although there might not actually be any real force guiding your price, people need to feel that there is.

FINDING YOUR MARKET

A basic part of marketing is actually knowing who your consumers are, which, in the faceless world of the Internet, can be difficult. You've probably noticed how many sites love to get you to register, along with some apparently useless information like your age and gender. It turns out, though, that is very valuable information. Finding a unique feature for your product and deciding the price will depend heavily on who would be interested in your product. This can often be quite intuitive. If you're selling earrings then it is most likely you will have a female market, but what age and what demographic? Some of this information can be found through research of other businesses selling similar products, but also using Etsy's statistics or Google analytics can be very helpful. You can, at the very least, see where your viewers are from and which of your products are most popular (views and sales might not be the same thing). Where a person lives can tell you a lot. If your boots are selling to people only in rural locations, you know something important about who and where your market is.

The age and gender of your customers can be important. A pair of earrings being sold by someone who looks young, and being modeled by a teenager, will not sell well to an older market, and, accordingly, younger people will not want products intended for a pensioner. There is a delicate balance between branding and tact: you want to target your audience, but you do not want to alienate others. You will also find that knowing your audience is vital in understanding where to market your product. If you make vegan boots, then you will have an easier time targeting sites that cater to people with ethical shopping on their minds instead of sites that treat ethical and less ethical products the same. Your audience will also tell you how much you can realistically charge and what questions a customer might have. If it is likely to be sold as a gift, your description might want to highlight a strong return policy or provide answers to as many questions as possible.

Even with market research and analytics at hand, it can be difficult to know exactly who is buying your products. One of the handy features on

Etsy is user reviews and feedback. You can look at your own items or similar items and look at the users that have left feedback and the types of items they generally buy and assess who they might be from that. Someone who buys many interesting items with not much practical purpose might use Etsy to buy gifts; someone who buys mostly beige trousers might be older. Try to make a note of what you find because it might not turn out to be the same as what you initially had thought. Consider something such as lingerie; it might seem obvious that since it is primarily for women, you would target the product entirely at women, but with market research you might find this strategy is not the most effective.

CREATING A BRAND

You know your price, you know your unique selling points or categories, and you know your target audience. The most important thing now is creating a brand. Some people resist the idea of a brand because it can seem restrictive or corporate. Nevertheless, a brand is all your customer is going to see, and you need to create a long-term business that people will keep returning to, this will require a brand. A brand does not have to be this soulless or boring ball-and-chain that forces you to always use the same kind of look and advertising copy. A good brand will sell you and your ideas to your customers.

What you should do in the beginning is figure out what your ideas are and where your brand will come from. Do you make quirky gifts? Do you make ethical clothing? Do you make good-quality practical clothing? If you just want to make a few nice things that people will hopefully buy that is fine, but that is not a business people can buy into. Discover what it is that drives you to sell and make that the theme you put everything around. Let's say you do make quirky gifts, you can easily work from that point and start having a brand that emphasizes this. You can make sure all of your pictures are fun (try using novelty models for your items or putting them in front of an interesting background), and then consistently use a voice that reflects you as the creator in everything that you do as part of your business.

A lot of brands work by having a mantra: the department store, Selfridges, claims it tries to 'surprise, amaze and amuse' its customers. In everything it does it will ask whether it is accomplishing those things, and if it does not then it will try to improve it. You can do something similar and then when you are creating any element of your business ask, "does this reflect my aim?" You need to make your brand wide enough that you can always meet your goals. If your aim is to make ethical clothing, then you can't always have branding that displays that so you will need something wider such as 'homemade'. Once you have the idea down you will then need to keep it central and when you want to add something new ask how you can make it fit into the brand you have. Try to pick a consistent logo, font, voice and, if possible, a color scheme. These simple things make you seem trustworthy and you will have something customers can buy into.

GETTING TO THE TOP OF A SEARCH ENGINE

Getting your marketing and image down is the most important first step in getting an Etsy business that will sell your products well into the future. Part of the reason why it is so important to have this ready in the beginning is that you need to put your market research and branding into your efforts to get high on a search engine. A search engine ranks you by how relevant it feels your content is to the keyword that has been put in, and also how relevant it will be to a user. How this works varies depending on the search engine. Google is currently more concerned with ensuring that a user gets content back that is more current and active. Etsy is more likely to put up matches that meet keywords. You will also be ranked on how well connected you are to other sites, especially how many other sites link to you. An Etsy product page is very similar to Google's pages. Some of the things you can do to promote a site will work on both Google and Etsy.

IMPROVING YOUR KEYWORDS

Keywords encompass several different things which will get picked up by search engines. This includes the titles, tags, keywords and Metadata that gets used on your site (the description that shows up below a link on a search engine). All of these things can get picked up when people are searching for something so you need to be there wherever possible.

The first thing you need to do is decide what your keywords are going to be. You want words that are popular, but the most desirable keywords are ones that carry the right meaning but there is not much competition in terms of other people with similar products. You can find this out using Google's Adwords tool which will let you type in phrases and it will provide you with an indication of how often they are searched and the competition for them. Remember that phrases get looked at in order, something such as 'small red earrings' will get searched for as 'small red' or 'red earrings', you want the best combination for your product that will get the right searchers to your site, but also will not have that much competition from other users and sites. You can also find popular keywords by simply beginning to type words into the Etsy search bar or Google's own search bar. Whatever you type in will match up with popular search terms.

Knowing what is popular is good, but to find the best popular words you need to be looking at the right words and phrases. For this, look around at other similar products and try to find out what their keywords are (look at the title and description for clues). Make a list of good phrases and try them out separately, then see which ones get the best results. This will take time, but after only a few weeks you will have an idea of what works well and what doesn't. Try to experiment with many different keywords and tags; you don't just have to use words that have to do with the item, but also things such as the season or the type of person that might want the item: 'Christmas stockings for Goths'.

USING YOUR KEYWORDS

Once you have found out which keywords and tags are best, you need to start using them. Obviously you can put them in the tag section of a product description, but you also need to have them in your product title and description, as well as your shop title and announcement. The first 66 characters of your shop title and the first 160 characters of your description or announcement will come up in a search engine, so make sure to include your shop's name and the keywords.

Spamming keywords will get picked up in a search engine and you will get penalized for this. What you need to do is use keywords naturally in the title and description, and make sure they are in correct search order. You will need to do this within copy that is intelligent and well-written. People will avoid anything that looks too amateurish. It is also important to note that your username will be included in search engines as well; it is a good tactic to have a username that is relevant to your product.

Try to vary your descriptions and titles if you can. This is smart for two reasons: Search engines will reject sites that are too similar and this could hurt your search engine ranking. It limits how often you can come up in different search engines, it will make you seem less relevant because all the sites would be the same. Don't worry about people missing similar items that they would like because of a different title, they will most likely be able to see them on your page.

The second reason has to do with how Etsy works. People search Etsy through many different sources on the site. They may go straight through browse, they may go through bigger categories like 'wedding', or they may look at the trending options. Having the same titles will mean you can only come up in the same place in all of these options, whereas a variation on your items may give you more success in different areas. It is also good to have quite a few products if you can (though it is better to have a few good quality products rather than many similar low-quality ones).

Lastly, make sure that all of your keywords are checked and kept up to date. You are not given leeway for things that are spelled incorrectly and most search engines correct the searcher's spelling so don't worry about needing to get keywords for poor spellers.

GETTING MORE LINKS

Search engines have changed over time and you will now get more credit for sites that show they are being used regularly or are popular. This means it is vital that you frequently add new content to your sites and keep them up to date. You can also get other sites to link to your page. It used to be that you could cheat this system slightly by just having huge lists of links to your sites, but this does not work as well anymore. You need to be linked to by sites that have their own unique visitors and you get more credit for being linked to by a bigger site.

You can create links to yourself via your own websites and social media, but this will limit you to only a handful of links that will only be as useful as you've grown those other sites. If you have a Facebook account with only a few friends and it isn't used much, linking to your own Etsy page is not going to help you a great deal.

You can still manipulate things such as Twitter to help develop stronger links to your site; many users will follow back for followers. If you use an app such as Tweet Deck you can monitor various trends and hash tags to see new posts. From there you can follow, re-tweet and interact with those users, most of who will likely follow you back. You can use other apps such as Just Unfollow to monitor who is following you back and who is not so that you can crop your followers to make sure they are active users who are happy to favorite content.

Using these methods, you can have a very high re-follow rate and have hundreds of followers within a short amount of time. If you interact with your followers, start up conversations, favorite their links and content, then they will do the same for you. This will help in a few ways. You will get views directly from Twitter users, and you will also get linked to from different followers for the same item. It is important to have followers that are in a field that is relevant to you such as the craft community that is very active online. Doing this will also give you good contacts in the field that might be relevant to you; it might also give you opportunities to submit your products for reviews.

There are similar opportunities with Facebook but it is often not as open to businesses promoting themselves. You are still able to promote yourself like that and with clever social media management you can use your business page to promote yourself. There are other options open to you as well. Pinterest is the go to website for Etsy users because it will allow you to post images to a captive audience, promoting yourself there. Becoming a big user could get your items and images circulating the internet quicker than you think.

Blogging is a strong option. You can set up your own blog fairly easily and try to become an expert in your field. If you are good at crafting something or you know a lot about vintage clothing, try to write articles and connect with others. You can also use sites like Yahoo answers or Quora to share your information and then link back to your sites. Remember to use your username whenever possible as this will all inevitably link back to Etsy. Many people find they enjoy this element of promoting themselves because they get to connect with members of the communities that you have an interest in. If you can get other bloggers to review your items, then you will be getting very good links to your site.

You should make sure to list your business on different sites like Google business so that your name gets around. It is important to remember that all of your sites and your general online presence are linked. If a few different things do well then it can bring up the rest of your online content. It's a positive feedback loop where the stronger one site gets, the stronger the sites it links to get. Bloggers, for example, will be keener on reviewing your products if you have a larger online following because it also helps them to get views.

Another option is within Etsy itself. If you interact with the community on forums to help them with their problems, then you will come up on search engines as a more active user. Being more active is always useful and will constantly give you more opportunities to grow. Interacting with others on Etsy will get people to look at your page more often and will encourage sales. Getting feedback for your sales is also useful because you will then have a host of new content from unique visitors.

Etsy does not have to be the entire source of sales for your product. You could also sell items on Amazon and eBay and then link to your full range on Etsy (keep in mind though that you don't want to spread yourself too thin or you will lose the homemade quality that Etsy prides itself on). You can sell your products through other outlets; try contacting different websites and sellers to see if they want to stock your product. If you promise them a small amount and make sure your brand is seen it can mean users will search for you afterwards. If you have a big enough product you might think about using coupon sites like Groupon to bring attention to your product as much as gaining sales.

PROMOTION

You now have a good brand that people will respond well to, people are able to find you easily on search engines and when looking for products like yours. You are now looking to further promote your products so they will get seen. Many of the options in the tips for promoting your site's links will also work as promotional aids but there are other things you can do to specifically promote your Etsy products.

One of the best ways to promote your site is with options Etsy has on its own site. Etsy's treasury is a great way to get onto the front page of Etsy and really show off your products and your brand. The treasury is a term that Etsy has given to what is a picture gallery of 16 of your items. You are able to make galleries of your own like this and have this featured on the homepage of your shop. This is a fantastic way to show off your products. You should make sure a clear theme emerges and there is a cohesive image given off by the entirety of your products. If your treasury looks good, then it can receive views and likes from users like any other page or feature you can have.

The exciting part of the treasury is that the elders of Etsy, its curators, sort through different profiles and look at different treasuries and if they choose yours it will be featured on the front page of the website and users can find your site. These curators and other members of the Etsy council also release a regular newsletter that highlights different products and members they feel reflect the Etsy spirit and show off charm and innovation. This means that you need to create a business that really revels in being handmade or vintage, and tries to connect with users and delivers them a good quality service. You will not receive much respect if you do not have impeccable customer service, which means responding to customers quickly, ensuring that customers know which product they are getting, and making sure that products are being sent on time and turning up in the best condition.

Becoming involved in the Etsy community is also very important. It brings you up on the radar of curators and creates more opportunities. You can join teams within the Etsy forum system. These teams tend to unify under skills such as metal work or buying certain vintage products. You may need to meet certain requirements to join a team, but many will allow you to join without any requirements. These will let you go into sub-forums where you can get help, provide help, and make contacts. You may also become more involved and start helping to run the teams. You may want to start some of your own workshops to increase your prestige and gain credibility.

ADVERTISING YOUR ETSY BUSINESS

Already there has been frequent mention of ways to advertise your business without any upfront financial cost, but there are also paid advertising options that you can use to promote your products and your business. Paying for advertisement work is debatable. It will depend on the types of items you sell and your business strategy. You obviously want to create as much income as quickly as possible; however, you may also be happier with a slower turnaround of products so you can lower your operation costs. In most cases it is advisable to try out these methods for yourself. Make a note of the number of views and the increase of sales that advertising gets you. Do not assume that just because you are paying, your adverts will give the correct message, that people will click on adverts, or that people will necessarily buy more if they do come to your site.

Etsy has the option of paying to have a listing promoted which you can get by bidding on the option for an ad so you come up at the top of a search result. You do this by putting in a maximum amount you will pay for advertising. There is an automatic auction that will give the advertising to the highest bidder. You have to pay for the times you get an ad click from a promoted link. You can play with this for a while and see what level of auction bid will get your product promoted. Since you only pay for getting an ad click you do not face the same risk as a lot of advertising options but it still does not guarantee you a sale. You may like to test this and take a gamble when you have a good product that is seasonal. You can choose whether you want to advertise individual products or your own business. Advertising your own products is usually an advertisement for your business, and vice versa, advertising your business will advertise your product.

You can leave on some lower bids if you wish and try them in different categories. You are best off having higher bids in more popular categories and using SEO to get your products higher in more niche categories. If you are going to pay to bid, and you bid a higher price, you should have good management of your products and your shop. You need to know when a product is going to sell well, when to stop paying for products that are not selling well, even with advertising, and which other products could really benefit from even higher placed results on the Etsy listing. It is important if you are going to pay to promote an item that you do all you can to make sure that people will click on it and that the item looks enticing from the image and description.

Pinterest is another method of promoting your business that has become more integrated with Etsy so that even the most novice user can combine the Pinterest and Etsy accounts. You can do this with the 1-click Pinterest promotion applications online which will immediately transfer all of your listings across and for a small fee they will ensure your products get views and attention. You should be cautious with any apps or solutions such as this because they may not give you genuine viewers or users coming to you. This might possibly increase your search engine ranking but remember that paying people to look at your products does not mean you will get more sales.

SEO INTRODUCTION

Etsy has become the go-to site for smaller sellers of craft items and vintage goods. It works so well as a platform because it favors the little guys and the unique products they want to sell. Unlike bigger online stores such as Amazon or eBay, when you shop with Etsy you know that people are not looking past you for brand names. Etsy is built to promote novel items and it gives you many tools to get your shop seen, whether by being featured on the front page, by paying for advertising, or by becoming a big part of the Etsy community. Etsy also gives you the option to increase the chances that your shop, and your products, will come up higher in a search engine. You do this by optimizing the online content you make for search engines, a process called Search Engine Optimization or SEO.

There is much mythology and misunderstanding when it comes to SEO. Some less-than-honest people are happy to sell you the idea that if they can get you to the top of a search engine they can make you rich. They tell you this because for a long time there was a mechanical process that could be exploited to get pages to the top of a search engine. They didn't want to tell you that being at the top of a search engine only mattered if people were searching for your products, or that people may still choose to overlook you.

Search Engine Optimization

Things have changed more recently, and search engines like Google now run on a more honest basis. Your site will only reach the top if Google sees it as having quality content. This means that in trying to optimize your content for search engines you will actually have to make products that people want. SEO is no longer a simple strategy for getting a high ranking artificially with lots of links and keywords. It is more like a marketing strategy that requires you to have a good brand. When it comes to an Etsy page you will have to work at getting your shop to the top of the Etsy search, but for this to have real power you will need to also get your products high up on Google, and also noticed in the wider world of the Internet.

Even though the process of SEO has gotten more complex, and requires more from you creatively, it is still made up of many simple processes. This book will tell you what SEO is and how it works for Etsy, how to increase your SEO ranking on Etsy and Google, and also how to mount a strategy that will keep your shop fresh and in a wider sphere of influence.

WHAT IS SEO?

The first thing to understand when trying to take over the world of search engines is how the things actually work. It may not be something you've thought about in depth before. You type in 'cats' and you get a list of results, and then you just go through them until you find an appealing one. But, how does a search engine choose which websites to include in its results, and how does it actually rank them?

You know from your own dealing with search engines that search engines don't just use straight forward systems of ranking. When you type in 'cats' there isn't a list of websites arranged alphabetically, or by when they were uploaded to the Internet, or when they were last edited. In fact, you'll find that most of the time the site you wanted will be included in one of the first few results you get. Search engines work by providing the most value to its user. If you type in 'cats' and get nothing but sponsored results you don't want, or you have to spend time going through pages of links, you'll avoid using that search engine again. A good search engine for a user is one that will put the sites that will be most relevant to their search at the top of a search results list.

This understanding is very important in both optimizing your content and in promoting your business. For SEO to have value you have to reach your audience. You should not be asking, "How can I cheat the system so that my content is at the top of a search engine?" You should be asking, "How do I tell a search engine that my content is going to be the most relevant content for a user that is looking for my type of content?" In the case of

Etsy, you are asking, "How can I tell a search engine that my products are the most relevant products for someone looking for 'silver earrings'?" Simply abusing a system will not get you your desired result because you don't just want to be seen; you want sales.

Search Engineoptimization

SEO

So how do you tell a search engine that your site is going to be the most relevant for a specific search term? If you take a site like Google it works by indexing all of the websites that it can find. Think of this as analogous to an index in a book. It finds content with something called a web crawler. This crawler scans web pages and looks at things such as their page titles, data, keywords on the site, information in images, and even things such as page layout. For a page to get crawled it will need to be easily seen in Internet terms. This means it needs to be linked to by an already indexed site or it needs to be added manually by a user to the search engine.

Once found in a crawl, that web page will be added to the search engine's index. When a word or query is made into a search engine it is held against the billions of sites that are indexed and the search engines ranking algorithm will decide which indexed pages are the most relevant. How does it decide what is relevant? Nobody really knows. The search engine gods don't tell us how their algorithms work, because if they did people would cheat the system and suddenly results would not be relevant to users and the search engine wouldn't be as powerful. So we are left to try out different rituals that please the search engine gods and we hope that what is working is not just coincidence.

There are some things we do know. In the past, keywords were very important; the more you had of a specific keyword, the higher you'd come up for that keyword. That's no longer quite the case, but obviously having the keyword in your content is vital, because it is what is ultimately connecting your content and the search results. This means you need to have careful and intelligent use of keywords, in the places of pages that web crawlers look at, such as the page title and the content itself.

The other important factor is links. Again, for a while building a link empire would make you king of your chosen keyword, but that is no longer the case. Having too many pointless links will not rank you higher. Now what is important is having links from sites that have strong levels of what is called page or domain authority. The domain authority is determined by the number of good links from other good websites (getting linked from Huffington Post is great, getting linked from a popular Facebook account is okay, getting linked from a spam website is bad), having a website that is easy to get around (pages that are not linked to enough can be hidden from search engines), and having content that people actually want to read and link to. There are other factors at play that fall out from having good content, such as how new content is, and how active a website is. Without those elements you would never see news stories at the top of a search engine.

The basic principles for optimizing content

So you know the basics of how a search engine works and you probably have a few ideas how to make your site better. The principles in this book will look mostly at Etsy shops. If you are using your personal website, there are many other steps you can take to increase your site's mapping and keywords and general SEO. Etsy does not allow for the same kind of optimization as your own personal site, but luckily that means you are on equal footing with other Etsy shops that face the same limits. Eventually you will want to extend your presence to your own site – if only for self-promotion. This is because by using just Etsy you are limited in your avenues for marketing and having your products higher in a search engine. Nevertheless, your Etsy page will get ranked on Google as will all of your individual products.

To do well in search engines you need a cohesive approach and you need to try to own a keyword. Think of this like marketing your brand, you need to own that brand for people to recognize it. You cannot compete with Coca Cola as the best cola drink; instead you need to be the best homemade cola drink or the best caffeine free cola drink. This principle applies here at a lower level as well, so that you can become the best of whatever unique set-up you feel you can dominate, even if that is just earrings made out of recycled aluminum cans.

You cannot own too many different keywords for the simple fact that you can't optimize content in that many different ways. You have limited space for keywords and you need links from sites that matter to your specific keyword. This means when building your business and choosing what to sell that you should keep your ideas connected with some uniformity. This does not mean you only need to sell shoes, for example, but that you should have something you can apply to many different products. This might be the material you make the products from, how you make it, or perhaps the special location where they are made.

It was said earlier that keywords didn't factor hugely in SEO anymore, but at its core a search engine is still looking for a specific keyword or phrase so you need to build around that. The keyword phrases you use on your page will determine which Google will pick up. You should also be clever with your username or shop name, so that it too could become something that Google will pick up and rank highly. If you have a common name it would be smart to use something that has a chance of easily standing out and coming to the top.

 It should seem clear now that increasing your SEO is just another facet of a marketing campaign. You choose the keywords or brand that you think will sell well, you create an enticing product, you start getting customers in and marketing your product on other sites and blogs who will link to your pages, you get your products seen on sites like Google shopping and Pinterest, and all of this adds to your page authority and your Google ranking.

The basic principle begins with the keywords, though. Later we will discuss where to place them on a page specifically for SEO.

How to find the best keywords and content for promotion

Choosing which keywords to use on your page is not quite as straightforward as it seems, and this is something that some SEO guides ignore because it is not quite such a predictable mechanical process. Firstly, it is important to note that the order of keywords matters to a search engine. Words that are next to each other rank together. So 'aluminum can earrings' will do well for 'aluminum can', and 'can earrings', but it will not do as well for 'aluminum earrings'. When you are choosing a keyword or phrase to adopt ensure that it bunches up well. The order in something such as a title or description matters as well. If you choose 'aluminum earrings', then a title such as 'one pair of fantastic homemade aluminum earrings' will not rate 'aluminum earrings' as the most important part of that title.

Picking the words for your phrase has to make a delicate balance between conveying the correct message or product, while also meeting the best niche in terms of keywords so you are getting words that are used the least by others, but will be searched the most by your customers. Take some time to look for products that are similar to yours, both on Etsy and on

Google. Try to see how quickly you can find a product you would want to buy, or that is fairly similar to what you have. Write down how you got there, and after how many different tweaks and searches. You'll likely find it was rarely just the first item that sprung up and that you had to change your search once or twice to get more specific.

keywords

exclusivity

professional

policy → SEO ← research

hardwork

links

optimization

Once you have some ideas of your own, test them out to see what is popular and what is trending. You can do this simply by starting to type them into Google and seeing what starts to pop up. You can also use tools like Google's keyword planner and wordtrackers keyword tool to see how popular an expression is, and more importantly, if it hits the sweet spot. Words that are searched frequently, but are not high in volume, come in what is known as the 'long tail' of searches. The first 30% of search results are made up of words like 'earring', but the remaining 70% of searches are covered by more unique phrases like 'aluminum stud earrings', which are searched far less. However, there is also less competition for them.

You should create a set of phrases that you can use to corner the market. You cannot use lots of hugely different keywords, but it is valuable to have your products listed slightly differently so you can cover different markets. Let's say you are making earrings, then you could try:

Soda Pop Earrings

Handmade Aluminum Earrings

Unique Gift Aluminum Earrings

Wedding Aluminum Earrings

Look for further synonyms to give you more ideas. People sometimes think they should try to be tricky with search engines, and include foreign spellings or misspellings but often this will not help you greatly. If you predict you will get a lot of customers from different parts of the world, however, then try to include the different variations that might come up for a word. Don't worry too much about an iteration of your product not doing quite as well. If handmade aluminum earrings does best, do not change all your products to this because you will start competing with yourself, and many users will find your other products through your page. The final step comes after implementing your SEO. You can then track how well a word does and decide which to keep and which to change or expand on.

How does SEO work for Etsy?

There are many transferable aspects for SEO that will work on different sites, and things that will rank your product higher on the Etsy search will also work for Google. However, the Etsy search engine is different than the algorithm that Google uses. It is more old fashioned in a way and it does not rely on the same level of networking and connectivity to big sites. Your choice of keywords and the layout of your site are very important to how well your site will rank within Etsy's own search engine, and it is not possible to cheat the system too much. This is because you cannot truly predict how customers will search for items (so getting to the top of the wrong item will not help), and spamming lots of keywords will seem very obvious to people looking at your products. You never want to lose sales for a higher search ranking.

The main way you will be listing your keywords is within the title and product description. Your shop and about information is important, but especially in the beginning people will be searching for your products and not you. So it is the product that will get seen in a search engine, and that is how you want it. To do this will require a mixture of the right keywords in titles, in the description, in tags on images and on your page, and with the correct categories.

Tags

Most of that will be familiar so just a word about tags and categories. There are literal tags that you input in a 'tag' section when listing a product. You can have up to 12 tags they can be up to 20 characters each.

You are not obliged to use all of the characters, and you cannot use punctuation or symbols in your character allowance. Etsy used to rank by how recent the products were, but it now does so by relevancy so using more characters (and words) is usually beneficial. It is useful to repeat the main keywords that will be in your title in your tags as well. Try to be mindful of the trends that are going on at that moment, if people are after vegan products then include that. Also be aware of the seasons around the world that might be relevant to your product. It might turn out that your style of jewelry is perfect for festivals or carnival season.

You do not want your tags to be too disparate in their content; it is always best to have close variations that are likely to come up. If you are selling the aforementioned aluminum earrings then tag them as 'gift earrings', 'aluminum studs', 'handmade earrings' etc. Avoid anything too wild or irrelevant to what you are actually selling. Vague terms like jewelry should be avoided if you have stronger, and more specific, tags in mind to be used. It's unlikely to really help you get searched. Don't panic about going for a specific customer. People searching for your specific items are looking for what you have to offer. This means that people finding your products want them.

There is another meaning for tags in the SEO world. Often tags are considered anything that will be picked up by a search engine crawler. Google pays particular attention to what are known as 'alt tags' which is the alternative text for an image on the page (if you put an image on a webpage and look at the HTML you will see this), and this is what is seen by the crawler robots and it has an impact on your ranking. On many websites you will change the tags of images so that they will be picked up by a crawler. For Etsy the title of listing automatically acts as the alt tag for an image. In the Etsy search, having more images won't impact your ranking, but for Google, having more images increases the number of tags that show up for your keywords.

Categories

Categories are not that important in terms of SEO because they do not actually alter where your site comes up on a search engine, since they are how your product is grouped rather than tagged in the engine. However, Etsy is moving closer to a model where users shop around by playing with categories and refine their search with these tools rather than manually adding in new words into the search engine such as 'wedding' or 'gift', if their initial search didn't result in what they wanted. This is a blessing really for the shop owner because it means you do not have to waste as many tags on things that categories will take care of. If somebody wants cheap earrings or earrings for weddings they will simply click on those categories and change the price range. This does mean though, that you have to think carefully about categories.

If you have lots of different products it is a good idea to try and get them into different categories, assuming they will fit there, so that you can cover a bigger range of users who might, for example, not think of your products for a wedding, but would nevertheless be interested. Categories should also factor into the keywords that you choose. You know you are going to become boxed into different categories and this will affect how people search for items. It may not be worth using tags for color, and becoming too niche might not work in your favor if a user can put in a search term like 'earrings' and simply reduce other products with categories. This means you need to be smart about your keywords because people might never get around to typing in a very specific search term. The only way to be sure you have the best keywords is to look at the stats and see which get you best ranked and the most views.

Product Titles

Titles are possibly the most important aspect in the SEO of your products because they hit a few different areas on Etsy. Your item title on Etsy fills the roles of different components that are used in tradition SEO. A search engine crawler determines what your page is about and matches it to search terms based on the outline it gleans from a few different factors, such as the titles and alt tags. It also includes the headings used on a page, In HTML terms there are headings ranging from H1 to H6. These are HTML tags and they tell a page what is the most important heading, with 1 being the most important. Generally, the different headings correspond to different sizes. If all heading tags are on the same keywords, then a search engine knows for certain what the page is about. With Etsy your item title is automatically your Heading 1 tag.

What this means is that your item title has to be very specific and on point because it has so much impact on the overall SEO ranking you have, and is placed in several places. For both Google and Etsy, you should try to have long tail keywords in the item titles.

Product description

After the title, the factor that really impacts your SEO is the description of your item. This is because the product description of an item becomes what is called the ' description' of your page. The description is the description displayed under a search result that tells a user what is going to be on the page they are about to click on. It is important that descriptions use keywords, but since people will actually be reading this they also need to have compelling copy. This is lucky because with Etsy a good product description is already vital. You will have to change your thinking slightly, though, because your description is made up of only the first 100 words of your description.

The first 100 words of your description can have quite a big impact on your ranking in the search engine. You will need to replicate the keywords that are in your item titles to ensure you appear as the most relevant to the search terms you have. Don't try to become too clever with long tail keywords here though. You may be able to become first with something quite obscure, but that won't be worth it if no one would search for it. One hundred words is not that much text so you should use the first 100 words to give a general description of the product without too much specific information. Just be sure to include the important keywords and any other vital information such as the size, style, type, volume, or color of the product.

 After you have done that, go in to more information about the product and answer questions a user would have without them having to ask. It might seem good to interact with a customer, but in reality you want them to buy first and not feel the need to ask questions. People generally do not wait around in the online world if they can find what they want without asking. It might seem like not many online shoppers do this, but consider the amount of times you have gone from site to site looking for the same product, only with a piece of vital information. If your product has that then you are more likely to grab the sale, especially if you are on an established site like Etsy where many people will have an account.

It is a good idea to keep some of your personal spark and your products branding in your advertising copy, but with a description you should try to balance that with a very simple and crisp description of your product. Also remember that you may be able to pick up a few extra keywords for a search engine here. You want a few very strong keywords throughout, but if you have the space in your description it is worthwhile having the color or anything specific. If it is patchwork or multi-colored it is good to have that in the description. It won't hugely affect the ranking, but with all things being equal between your product and another identical one, this small word in the description could put the ranking in your favor.

Other content on your shop

Your shop and the features on it are also searched by Google's crawler so it is worth using them to their full advantage. You won't be able to actually increase the ranking on an individual product page with your shop information but you can make your shop rank higher. The shop page works like any other product page. The name works as the page title, the heading and as the alt tags for any images you have on the page. The shop description's first 100 words work as the Meta description for the shop. If you can try to have a word in the title that could work as a keyword itself, if you can't think of a name that works well with a keyword, or you already have a name for your business, then try to use your Etsy page to promote it.

It will be much easier to get views for an Etsy page than a personal website because users have a very obvious reason to visit it, they want your product. You also have a policies page which will be included in Google's crawler. This page is excellent for putting in your business page several times if you write it correctly. Make sure not to go overboard though. You might get flagged as a cheater. The stronger your shop is in its domain authority the better it will be if you link to your own content from it in future. It also helps to have a professional looking business if you want to take Etsy seriously.

Favorites and Treasury

These are the last two big features of Etsy that can impact on SEO in a very direct way. The first is favorites, which is where a user sends a heart your way and pins some of your products to their profile. This is good for getting out in the Etsy world by including you on the sites of others and also by being viewed in the feeds of others. It's likely that more active users are the ones who will grant you a heart so it can work out by spreading their charity further. If you have lots of friends or family using Etsy, then ask them to favorite your page (be clear so they don't just bookmark the actual page). If you become more active on the Etsy forums and join teams or groups, you might find you can favorite other shops for a favorite in return.

The second large feature is the treasury option. This is just Etsy's rather fancy word for a gallery that you can attach to your shop's page. Things like this are free SEO points for your shop, and they look good as well. The treasury is an important reminder about how vital it is to have good products that are presented well. A good treasury with inviting pictures is a very powerful marketing tool. The images are also checked by the crawler, but more importantly, these images might end up being featured on the front page. Doing well on Etsy requires a holistic approach that considers how your shop fits in. It is also good to have a non-cynical attitude and to try to get into the spirit of Etsy. Having the mindset that you want to be part of the community, rather than just to make money, will ultimately make you more successful. That is why people come to Etsy after all.

HOW TO GET YOUR SITE SEEN

Aims for this chapter: Discussing whether you should pay for advertising – learning how to market a product in the online world.

Paid advertising

SEO usually refers to non-paid for advertising, because if you pay you don't really need to optimize your content. It will already be listed. On Etsy these are called promoted listings. This feature works by you placing a bid on how much you would be willing to pay for each click your advert would receive. You can promote both your own business and an individual product. Promoting one will usually result in the other also being promoted. Once you have placed this bid it is taken through to an auction for the term you have chosen, whichever bidder has the highest bid on an item will get that advertising spot for the day.

Whether or not you want to use paid advertising is up to your preferences. The time it might take you to really optimize your content and keep on top of it might be better used just paying for the advertising space. Remember though, you are charged for clicks, not sales, so you are guaranteed nothing. People also tend to be averse to paid adverts on the Internet after years of abuse from advertisers. Yet, people do choose to use these adverts. It might be worth putting in a low bid just to see if it makes a difference in the event that you do win. When using these make sure to check if your sales increase. With paid advertising you can do much better in the bigger keywords. If your product is inherently unique, however, it is unlikely to be truly necessary to pay for advertisement.

Marketing in the online world

There are several ways to market your products online for free that will have an impact on your SEO. Most of these are relevant for your Google ranking rather than your Etsy one which is more traditional in its approach. The sister website for Etsy is Pinterest. Many users are made once one of their products becomes popular on Pinterest and from there it can catch the attention of bloggers or even fashion or home magazines. The key to doing well on Pinterest is to keep networking with new users to create innovative and interesting products that you photograph in a captivating way. Many SEO tips for Pinterest are similar to other sites in getting to the top but it also has its own unique set of rules.

Getting your Pinterest site highly ranked is not entirely essential; you just need to get it seen by the right people who may then link back to your Etsy account. Since you can link from an item on Pinterest back to Etsy there is also space for a strong backlink from a page with good authority if you can grow your Pinterest site. Pinterest is just the surface of what you can do with social media. The other big three sites you will want to use are Twitter, Facebook and a personal blog.

A blog can be set up easily with a site like Wordpress. You can either host it on Wordpress or host it with your own provider. If you host it yourself then the SEO options increase significantly, but doing it through Wordpress will also give you lots of advantages. The key to doing well here is to keep creating good content about your products. Whatever it is that is your unique selling point of your item, try to turn yourself into a master of it with interesting articles. Try to connect to other users by commenting on their articles and trying to guest blog on each other's pages. Try to write articles based on what Google says is trending and link to your Etsy page as much as possible without appearing desperate. The idea is to get the best and most active content you can linking to your Etsy page.

You can compound all of this activity with social media. Growing a Twitter or Facebook account is fairly simple. Many users on Twitter will trade a like for a like and by using applications like Tweet Deck you can see which items are using hash tags that are relevant to what you are creating and selling on Etsy. The value of this type of marketing is questionable in terms of making sales, but in terms of SEO it is good to have followers that will backlink to you in exchange for likes, favorites and re-tweets. Remember to keep active on these sites and to keep making good content.

KEEPING AHEAD OF THE GAME

The last step in creating a good SEO strategy is to prepare for the future, because it is a process that keeps evolving, so you need to keep ahead of it. Using applications from Goggle and Etsy, you can keep track of the different views that your pages get and where you are getting viewers from. You should pay regular attention to these figures so you know what works and what doesn't. So you can know at what times of the year different customers are interested in buying your products. You can decide which products need refreshing and where your SEO strategy needs to be updated.

 Don't be afraid to make riskier decisions in terms of SEO because the rules are not entirely written and you may find a new way of promoting your products that no one else has thought of yet. Keep a note of what changes you made and how the year went in order to plan for the years ahead.

You now know some of the most fundamental tricks and tips for success on Etsy; the key to always being ahead of the competition is to ensure that you are always evolving your system of advertising, promotion, marketing and internet exposure. Always keep your goals at the heart of what you are doing and keep the quality of your products and your business practice to a first rate standard. If you implement all you have learned and you have a good product, there is no reason why you cannot have success with Etsy.

Once you have the basics of SEO down for a smaller project like an Etsy page, maintaining a good search ranking requires constant vigilance of how you are ranking, and how your stats are playing out. With intelligent use of tags and keywords, as well as good quality products and a full marketing campaign that stretches across the reaches of social media, there is no reason that you cannot have a successful Etsy shop with a multitude of viewers and, it is hoped, many many customers.

CONCLUSION

There are many reasons for someone to open a business of their own. Personal reasons, professional reasons, frustration reasons, it does not matter. What matters is the ability to actually initiate the procedure to open up the business and the capability to maintain a sufficient level of services and products so that the individual who opened the business can keep it up and running for as long as possible.

An individual that seeks to begin a business in a traditional brick and mortar shop needs an abundance of capital or sufficient financing to cover the expenses of the rent, the initial equipment, the advertisement, the Internet site, the proper arrangements to maintain the safety and security regulations imposed by the relevant law, the initial stock, and sufficient funds to survive on until the new shop begins to return adequate profits.

This capital is slightly mitigated if the same individual decides to open an e-shop instead of a classic shop. Funds are still required for the person or persons who will design and bring the Internet site to life (assuming that the individual in question does not have the knowledge to build it on their own). Funds will be needed for the specialists who will handle the Internet marketing and for those who will be responsible for the techniques that will bring the new site to the top of the list of the organic results of the search engines.

Etsy was created for the purpose of offering the buyers the opportunity to buy directly from the people who actually design and produce goods. They provide unique items and vintage pieces, and allow the sellers to acquire a much larger audience and a much wider market place than the traditional craft fairs.

Buyers have the opportunity to find items from all over the world that they would otherwise not have access to, while sellers can set up their own individual enterprise based on the platform provided by Etsy with minimal effort and by making use of the tools that Etsy provides for this purpose.

For the sellers it is a relatively easy overall process that can yield results if they are patient and follow the rules that Etsy has imposed. They do well if they implement some rather simple strategies and tactics that have been time tested again and again for their effectiveness, while avoiding the traps and the usual mistakes that go with the venture.

It does not mean that the rest of the principles that govern business transactions, either of the traditional style or through the e-commerce world, cease to apply. Sellers are still required to show professionalism, show that they are serious about what they are doing and be courteous to their customers, regardless whether they are going just for a bit of additional income or for a main source that will allow them to quit their current jobs.

If you are one of these individuals and you have read carefully what you need to know, what you need to do and have decided that opening up a shop by taking advantage of the platform that Etsy offers is the best option for you, all we can say is -- welcome to the world of Etsy.

16031992R00069

Printed in Poland
by Amazon Fulfillment
Poland Sp. z o.o., Wrocław